my many emotions

Sadness

Cherry Lake Press

Published in the United States of America by Cherry Lake Publishing Group
Ann Arbor, Michigan
www.cherrylakepublishing.com

Reading Adviser: Beth Walker Gambro, MS, Ed., Reading Consultant, Yorkville, IL
Content Adviser: Emily Fragapane, M.Ed., Ed.S., Nationally Certified School Psychologist, RYT200
Book Designer: Jennifer Wahi
Illustrator: Jeff Bane

Photo Credits: © P-fotography/Shutterstock.com, 5; © Stock-Asso/Shutterstock.com, 7; © Alexander_Safonov/Shutterstock.com, 9; © Forewer/Shutterstock.com, 11; © LightField Studios/Shutterstock.com, 13; © J.Dream/Shutterstock.com, 15; © Serenko Natalia/Shutterstock.com, 17; © GOLFX/Shutterstock.com, 19; © SeventyFour/Shutterstock.com, 21; © fizkes/Shutterstock.com, 23; Cover, 2-3, 6, 14, 22, 24, Jeff Bane

Cherry Lake Press is an imprint of Cherry Lake Publishing Group.

Library of Congress Cataloging-in-Publication Data

Names: Devera, Czeena, author. | Bane, Jeff, 1957- illustrator.
Title: Sadness / by Czeena Devera ; illustrated by Jeff Bane.
Description: Ann Arbor, Michigan : Cherry Lake Publishing, [2021] | Series: My many emotions | Includes index. | Audience: Grades K-1
Identifiers: LCCN 2021004949 (print) | LCCN 2021004950 (ebook) | ISBN 9781534186941 (hardcover) | ISBN 9781534188341 (paperback) | ISBN 9781534189744 (pdf) | ISBN 9781534191143 (ebook)
Subjects: LCSH: Sadness--Juvenile literature. | Emotional intelligence--Juvenile literature. | Social learning--Juvenile literature.
Classification: LCC BF575.S23 D48 2021 (print) | LCC BF575.S23 (ebook) | DDC 155.4/124--dc23
LC record available at https://lccn.loc.gov/2021004949
LC ebook record available at https://lccn.loc.gov/2021004950

Printed in the United States of America
Corporate Graphics

table of contents

About the author: Czeena Devera grew up in the red-hot heat of Arizona surrounded by books. Her childhood bedroom had built-in bookshelves that were always full. She now lives in Michigan with an even bigger library of books.

About the illustrator: Jeff Bane and his two business partners own a studio along the American River in Folsom, California, home of the 1849 Gold Rush. When Jeff's not sketching or illustrating for clients, he's either swimming or kayaking in the river to relax.

Have you ever seen a rain cloud? It's gray. It looks heavy. Now, **imagine** a rain cloud inside your body. That's **Sadness**.

How would you describe Sadness?

Sadness is quiet. It can **linger** for a while or suddenly **appear**.

Sadness can come with changes. Like when a friend moves. Or when you get a new teacher.

Sadness can come with **loss**. Like when a pet runs away. Or when a family member leaves after a visit.

Have you ever cried during a movie? That's okay! Seeing someone hurt can make you sad. Even if it's just on a screen.

How does Sadness feel to you?

Your body might feel heavy. Your head might hurt. Your throat and eyes might be sore.

You might want to be left alone. Or you might cry for a while. These are normal **reactions**. Sadness should be **expressed** and not bottled up.

Everyone feels sad sometimes. It means you care. But Sadness shouldn't last forever.

Being near other people can help. Close your eyes and take a deep breath. Imagine something that makes you feel better.

Remember, it's okay to feel Sadness. Ask for help when you need it. You're not alone.

glossary

appear (uh-PIHR) to show up

expressed (ek-SPRESSED) showed feelings or thoughts by saying, doing, or writing something

imagine (i-MAJ-uhn) to picture something in your mind

linger (LIN-gur) to be slow in leaving

loss (LOSS) when something is lost

reactions (ree-AK-shuhns) behaviors or responses to something

sadness (SAD-nuhss) the state of feeling unhappy or helpless

index